# take it to the hoop, Magic Johnson

By **Quincy Troupe**

Illustrated by **Shane W. Evans**

 JUMP AT THE SUN
**Hyperion Books for Children**
New York

take it
to the

# hoop,

"magic"
johnson,

take the ball dazzling down the open lane

herk & jerk & raise your

six-foot, nine-inch frame

into air sweating screams
of your neon name

"Windex" Johnson

"magic" johnson, nicknamed "Windex"

Mary-Marie Askins

Benjamen Bajeedah

Christophe Bushemi

Betty Evans

JungSung Kim

Clarence Lynn

Lee Michael

Warren Vance

Paulette Walter

way back in high school
'cause you wiped glass backboards so clean,
where you first juked & shook,
wiled your way to glory

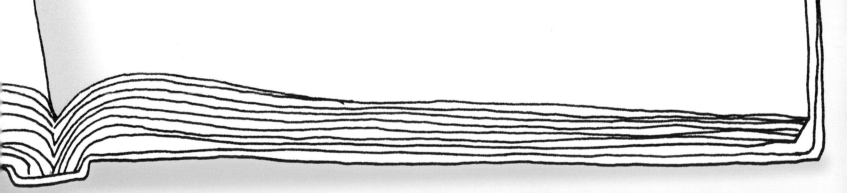

*a new*-style fusion of Shake 'n Bake
energy, using everything possible,
you created your own space to fly through—

any moment now
we expect your wings to spread
feathers for that spooky takeoff
 of yours

then, **shake** & **glide** & **ride** up in space
till you hammer home a clothes−lining deuce off glass
**now,**
come back down with a **reverse** **hoodoo** gem
off the spin & stick in **sweet**, popping
nets clean from **twenty** feet, right side

so put
the **ball**
on the
**floor again,**
"**magic**"

s l i d e the dribble behind your back,

ease it deftly between your bony stork
legs, head **bobbing** everwhichaway

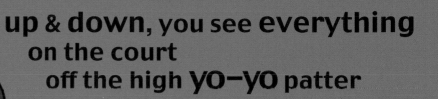

**up & down,** you see **everything**
on the court
off the high **yo-yo** patter

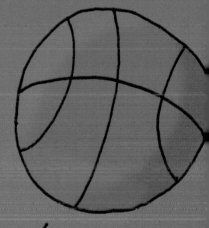

**stop** & **go** dribble
you thread a needle—rope pass sweet home

now, lead the fastbreak,
hit **worthy** on the fly

now, **blindside** a pinpoint
behind-the-**back** pass
for two more off the fake,
looking the other way,
you raise off-balance into
electric space
sweating chants of your
name

turn, 180 degrees off the
move, your legs scissoring
space
like a swimmer's
yo—yoing motion in
deep water
stretching out now
toward free **flight**
you double-pump
through human trees
**hang in place**

slip the ball into
your **left** hand

then deal it like a las vegas card dealer off squared glass
into nets, living up to your singular **nickname**

so "bad" you cartwheel the crowd
toward frenzy, wearing now your
electric smile, neon as your name

in victory, we suddenly sense your
glorious uplift, your urgent need to be

# champion

& so we cheer with you,
rejoice with you for this
quicksilver, **quicksilver**,
**quicksilver** moment of fame

so put
the **ball**
on the
**floor again,**
**"magic"**

**juke & dazzle,
Shake 'n Bake
down the lane**

take the sucker to the hoop,
**"magic" johnson,**

recreate

reverse

hoodoo

gems

**off the spin**

deal alley–oop **dunkathon**
magician passes
now, **double-pump**,
**scissor**, vamp through space

hang in place

& deal the roundball like the **juju** man that you am like the sho–nuff **shaman** that you am, **"magic,"** like the sho-nuff spaceman you am

For my grandchildren, Amina Grace, André-El, Courtney, Crystal,
Jonathan, Lillian, and Samuel, and my youngest son, Porter
—Q.T.

Thank you, GOD.
Dedicated to all of my aunts and uncles
for helpin' me "Take it to the hoop!"
—S.W.E.

the end.

Printed in Hong Kong
First edition
1 3 5 7 9 10 8 6 4 2

This book is set in Charcoal.
Library of Congress Cataloging-in-Publication Data
Troupe, Quincy.
Take it to the hoop, Magic Johnson/ Quincy Troupe ; illustrated by Shane Evans.–1st ed.
p. cm.
Summary: A poetic celebration of Magic Johnson and his quicksilver moments of
triumph on the basketball court.
ISBN 0-7868-0510-2 (trade) – ISBN 0-7868-2446-8 (library)
1. Johnson, Earvin, 1959–Juvenile poetry. 2. Basketball players–Juvenile poetry.
3. Afro-Americans–Juvenile poetry. 4. Basketball–Juvenile poetry. 5. Children's poetry,
American. [1. Johnson, Earvin, 1959–Poetry. 2. Basketball–Poetry. 3.
Afro-Americans–Poetry. 4. American poetry.] I. Evans, Shane, ill. II. Title.

PS3570.R63 T35 2000
811'.54–dc21
00-020407

Visit www.jumpatthesun.com